D1125217

611 Ways To Boost Your Self-Esteem

Bryan Robinson, Ph.D.
and
Jamey McCullers, R.N.

Publisher: Health Communications, Inc.
            3201 S.W. 15th Street
            Deerfield Beach, Florida 33442-8190

Cover design by Andrea Perrine Brower
Cover quilt "FAN-TASY" by Pat Reep
Photo courtesy of American Quilter's Society, Paducah, Kentucky

Introduction

Life is full of ups and downs and, at one time or another, all of us feel downtrodden or blue. Everyone wants to live a happy life. But why are so many of us miserable so much of the time, constantly searching for inner peace with little success? Because we're looking for it in the wrong places.

An ancient tale about Nasrudin, who lost his house key on the way home one night, illustrates this point. Nasrudin was down on all fours under the street lamp searching frantically when a stranger came by and asked him what he was looking for. Nasrudin told him that he had lost the key to his house. So the stranger, being a kind man, got down on his hands and knees and helped look for it. After hours of searching with no success, the stranger asked, "Are you sure you dropped the key in this spot?" Nasrudin said, "Oh, no! I dropped it way over there in that dark alley." Frustrated, the stranger asked angrily, "Then why are you looking for it here?" Nasrudin replied, "Because the light's better here under the street lamp."

Some of us are like Nasrudin, spending our lives looking in the wrong places for our self-esteem. We keep getting involved in unhealthy relationships that hurt us, we resist change and cling to sameness, we want most in life what we cannot have and are blind to the riches we already possess. We have learned to be victims, to be ruled by fear, to feel unworthy and to look for someone or something outside ourselves to make us happy.

What we need to realize is that self-esteem is a state of mind. When we have negative attitudes toward ourselves, we limit our lives every second we breathe without even realizing it. But by changing our thinking we can boost our self-esteem.

This book helps you to look within and examine who you are with a new frame of reference so that you can transform your life into a happy, fulfilling one.

If you are a people pleaser, if you are driven by "shoulds," "oughts" and other self-defeating messages; if you always put others' needs before your own, living your life for everyone but yourself, this book can help. Here you will discover 611 positive steps that can help you view your life in a different way, see how special you are and recognize all the things you have for which you can be grateful.

These 611 self-esteem builders give you new direction. They will guide you through each day with easy-to-apply reminders that show you how to empower yourself and restore the meaning and quality that bring balance to your life.

Bryan Robinson
Jamey McCullers
December 1993

1. *Remind yourself often that one is a whole number.*

2. *When faced with negative situations, try to look for the positive.*

3. *Sing in the car on the way to work.*

4. *If you don't work, get a job — or find something you enjoy doing — and sing on the way to doing it.*

5. *If you think you cannot sing, sing anyway.*

6. *Make cans instead of cannots.*

7. *Don't use a flame thrower on others when you live in a paper house.*

8. *Be a part of life instead of apart from it.*

9. *Satisfy the urge to change someone else by changing yourself.*

10. *Include yourself when you're thinking of some of your favorite people.*

11. *Value loyalty over royalty.*

12. *Put yourself up instead of down.*

13. *Surround yourself with people who affirm and respect you.*

14. *Avoid putting everyone else's needs before your own.*

15. *Know yourself.*

16. *Be yourself.*

17. *Love yourself with no strings attached.*

18. *Look for the upside of your life when all you can see is the downside.*

19. *Learn to be comfortable in your own skin instead of wishing you were in someone else's.*

20. *See friends instead of enemies on the faces of strangers.*

21. *Throw a party instead of a fit.*

22. *Get outside at least once a day, no matter how bad the weather.*

23. *Live by the adage, "Nobody can walk over you if you're not lying down."*

24. *Don't compromise yourself to win someone else's favor.*

25. *When you feel unloved, find someone for whom to do a loving deed.*

26. *Be a kid again.*

27. *Replace pessimism with optimism.*

28. *Have someone to confide in.*

29. *Be there for someone else.*

30. *When someone gives you a compliment, take time to hear it before returning the favor.*

31. *Spend time with upbeat people.*

32. *Take care of your body.*

33. *Remind yourself that denial is not a river in Egypt.*

34. *Refrain from "shoulding" on yourself; replace the word "should" with "could."*

35. *Instead of saying "yes" when you mean "no," say "no" when you mean "no."*

36. *When you fail, remember that success is built on failure.*

37. *Let someone else buy your dinner for a change.*

38. *Be happy instead of snappy.*

39. *Set goals to work toward.*

40. *Let go of other people's opinions and learn to please yourself.*

41. *Use a kind word when someone else has a sour attitude.*

42. *Suit yourself once in a while.*

43. *Learn to enjoy your own company.*

44. *Have a favorite color.*

45. *When life overwhelms you, take it one day and step at a time.*

46. *Treat yourself to a good time instead of waiting for someone else to do it.*

47. *Tell jokes.*

48. *Play* Trivial Pursuit.

49. *Make sure your joy equals your sadness.*

50. *In a give-and-take relationship, make sure you're not doing one more than the other.*

51. *See your human limitations as strengths instead of weaknesses.*

52. *Look for the gain in all of your losses.*

53. *Snuggle into a warm and cozy place and read a good book.*

54. *When you're forgiving others, don't forget to include yourself.*

55. *Be a survivor of life instead of a victim of it.*

56. *Develop your spiritual side.*

57. *Set healthy boundaries with others.*

58. *Don't put yourself first all the time.*

59. *Don't put yourself last all the time.*

60. *Ask "What's right?" instead of "What's wrong?"*

61. *Learn to receive as much as you give.*

62. *Write down all the things you dislike about yourself in one column and those you like in another. Make sure your two lists are equal in length.*

63. *Accept the things you cannot change.*

64. *Change the things you can.*

65. *Know the difference between the things you can and cannot change.*

66. *Spend quality time alone with yourself on a regular basis.*

67. *Develop a favorite hobby or pastime.*

68. *Treat yourself as you would your best friend.*

69. *Do something special just for yourself.*

70. *Let your anger out in constructive ways instead of carting it around everywhere you go.*

71. *Take a personal inventory and make a list of all your strengths.*

72. *Don't be anybody's doormat.*

73. *Love yourself and your neighbor.*

74. *See the hourglass as half full instead of half empty.*

75. *Treat yourself the way you want others to treat you.*

76. *Wiggle your toes in sand or mud.*

77. *Plan for the future but live in the present.*

78. *Accept your love handles, grey hair and everything else about yourself exactly as you are.*

79. *March to the beat of your own drum.*

80. *Swallow your pride instead of letting it devour you, and don't throw it up in someone else's face.*

81. *Develop an internal relationship with yourself.*

82. *Don't become intimately involved with crisis junkies.*

83. *Aim for progress, not perfection.*

84. *Ask yourself what you can learn from obstacles that are put in front of you.*

85. *Teach yourself to look for the merits instead of the flaws in every situation.*

86. *Always have more than one choice.*

87. *Develop a favorite hobby or pastime.*

88. *Avoid shaming yourself.*

89. *Think three positive thoughts about yourself before falling asleep at night and before getting out of bed each morning.*

90. *Get the slogan right: "Misery is optional, not optimal."*

91. *Be part of the solution, not part of the problem.*

92. *Accept life instead of resisting it.*

93. *Start seeing yourself as responsible for your life instead of at the mercy of it.*

94. *Expect the best that life has to offer.*

95. *Pay attention to "what is" instead of "what if."*

96. *Don't take yourself too seriously.*

97. *Don't be misguided into believing that changing your hair color, finding a different companion, rearranging the furniture or moving somewhere else will raise your self-esteem.*

98. *Surround yourself with people who bring out the best in you.*

99. *Avoid people who point out your faults all the time.*

100. *Add life to your days instead of days to your life.*

101. *Think about what you would have liked your parents to say and do but didn't; then say and do those things for yourself.*

102. *Think of one good thing you can say about yourself each day.*

103. *Choose your career wisely, making sure it's something you enjoy and is one in which you can feel good about yourself.*

104. *Live your life for yourself instead of for everyone else.*

105. *Let someone who is in a hurry go ahead of you in the grocery store line.*

106. *Go easy on yourself when you make mistakes.*

107. *Learn to feel more comfortable living on top than living the life of an underdog.*

108. *Turn lemons into lemonade.*

109. *Avoid magnifying little things to look bigger than they actually are.*

110. *Give yourself credit when it is due.*

111. Instead of trying to change someone or something, change your attitude about them.

112. Be open and spontaneous.

113. Learn to ask for what you want.

114. Watch the sun set.

115. Look for your own human good.

116. Apologize, don't rationalize.

117. *Cross each bridge as you come to it.*

118. *Don't burn your bridges behind you.*

119. *Cook a new recipe.*

120. *Negotiate, don't infuriate.*

121. *Use hope if you want to cope.*

122. *Look for the light at the end of the tunnel.*

123. *Complete just one item on your to-do list when you feel like procrastinating.*

124. *Let your hair down.*

125. *Value communication over justification.*

126. *Cushion your life so that you have space to stretch and breathe and to live moment to moment.*

127. Don't let others' skepticism divert you from your own truth.

128. Speak up for yourself.

129. Treat yourself with the same dignity and respect you give others.

130. *Don't trick yourself into believing that worrying will fix tomorrow's burdens. It steals today's strength.*

131. *Define your importance by your character, not by your accomplishments.*

132. *Never give your personal power to another human being.*

133. As you change, have patience with yourself because change is gradual and takes time.

134. Don't let the fear of what others think cause you to do things you don't want to do.

135. Have a candlelight dinner, even if you're dining alone.

136. *Accomplish what needs doing one at a time without worrying about the mountain of nonessentials.*

137. *Let your grief out by crying, pounding on a pillow, writing it out or telling a friend or counselor.*

138. *Remove yourself from unhealthy situations quietly and with love.*

139. Play.

140. Balance your logic with intuition because, in the words of Tagore, "A mind all logic is like a knife all blade. It makes the hand bleed that uses it."

141. When you feel downtrodden, remember the words of Eleanor Roosevelt, who said, "No one can make you feel inferior without your consent."

142. *Admit when you are wrong without condemning yourself or covering up your mistakes.*

143. *Rock the boat once in a while.*

144. *Avoid trying to fix someone else's life when yours is crumbling around your feet.*

145. *Learn to give and take without compromising who you are.*

146. *Never feel more comfortable with criticism than with praise.*

147. *Be assertive, not aggressive.*

148. *Choose your career based on what you* want *to do, not what you* have *to do.*

149. Accept compliments.

150. Instead of trying to figure out what others want you to be like, figure out what you want to be like.

151. Heed the advice of Lao Tzu, who said, "The journey of a thousand miles begins with but a single step."

152. *Stand up for what you believe.*

153. *Give yourself pep talks before challenging situations and after a big letdown.*

154. *Satisfy the urge to change someone else by changing yourself.*

155. *Meditate, don't medicate.*

156. *Have an attitude of gratitude.*

157. *Find your unique qualities and treasure what is special about yourself.*

158. *Explore a new area of interest.*

159. *Try line dancing.*

160. *Subscribe to uplifting magazines that give you tips for feeling good about yourself.*

161. *Climb a tree.*

162. *Write yourself a letter expressing how you feel about yourself.*

163. *Be calm in the presence of hysteria and watch the tone of the situation turn completely around.*

164. *Hit the middle of the road between self-centeredness and self-neglect.*

165. *Find a quiet place to go at the end of the day to sit and reflect inward.*

166. *Let go of anyone or anything in your life to which you have been clinging and they will come back to you in one form or another.*

167. *Don't blame your inner upset on outside causes.*

168. See people's faults as their wounds and have compassion instead of anger.

169. Laugh at least once a day.

170. Open a door for someone else.

171. Don't put your life on hold waiting for someone else to catch up.

172. Stop judging and criticizing yourself with self-talk.

173. Let go of negative, self-defeating thoughts to make room for positive, uplifting ones.

174. Engage in positive self-talk, especially when you are feeling blue or downtrodden.

175. *Make things happen in your life instead of waiting for them to happen to you.*

176. *Play penny poker.*

177. *Get a pet that will return your love a thousandfold.*

178. *Wrestle on the floor with your dog.*

179. *Give yourself three affirmations a day.*

180. Give long, warm hugs.

181. Never live your life according to what is right for someone else.

182. Spend your energy being *the right person* instead of finding *the right person.*

183. Be a nonconformist.

184. See your imperfections as part of your human perfection.

185. Do the thing that scares you the most and the fear will lose its power over you.

186. Share in other people's joy.

187. Image prosperity in your life.

188. *Realize that you cannot give to others something that you haven't given to yourself.*

189. *Be practical instead of academic.*

190. *Be choosy about the kinds of situations you put yourself in.*

191. *Pay as much attention to what you've accomplished as you do to what still needs to be done.*

192. *Praise yourself when you succeed* and *when you fail.*

193. *Have time just for yourself once in a while, even if you're in an intimate relationship.*

194. *Have a dinner party.*

195. *If you build walls between yourself and others, figure out what hurt you are protecting yourself from.*

196. Eat healthy foods.

197. Choose your feelings instead of using someone else as a barometer for how you feel.

198. Buy yourself a stuffed animal.

199. Pay attention to yourself when you feel you are being neglected.

200. Take pride in your triumphs but also acknowledge your shortcomings.

201. Reclaim that part of yourself that you put on the sidelines because you felt you didn't deserve happiness.

202. Ask for a hug when you need one.

203. Exercise daily.

204. *Believe that you can do anything you set your mind to.*

205. *Be able to distinguish past hurts from present situations.*

206. *Be willing to put effort into your relationships to make them worthwhile.*

207. *Have the capacity to be happy when someone else is sad.*

208. Ride the waves on a raft.

209. Focus on wanting what you have instead of on having what you want.

210. Learn when to speak and when to remain silent, when to step in and when to step aside.

211. *Accept responsibility for your actions regardless of the outcomes.*

212. *Think of someone whom you have condemned, criticized or treated unkindly and, in your heart or face-to-face, make amends to them.*

213. *Invent new solutions to old problems after wearing out old solutions that you know don't work.*

214. *Sit by a crackling fire and toast marshmallows.*

215. *Give your seat to an older adult on the bus.*

216. *Take a seat when someone offers you one.*

217. *Accept change with open arms.*

218. *Don't let others use their acceptance of you as blackmail to get their way.*

219. Buy yourself a new outfit.

220. Have a mind of your own.

221. Establish harmony and balance in your life.

222. Be honest about your capabilities instead of exaggerating your successes and hiding your shortcomings.

223. Be calm when someone else is hysterical.

224. When you overcome barriers, give yourself the credit you deserve in order to build your confidence.

225. Make conscious choices that put you in charge of your life.

226. Walk on a deserted beach and collect seashells.

227. Give your time to charities.

228. Make it a point to meet one new person a week.

229. Smile a little.

230. Smile a little more.

231. Love yourself unconditionally, no matter what.

232. *Remind yourself that only inner conditions — not outer conditions — can make a difference in your self-esteem.*

233. *Stop going back to the same people for the same rejections.*

234. *Be a composer of your life as a musician would compose a symphony — with notes.*

235. Be strong-minded and softhearted.

236. Realize that the way people treat you is more a reflection of how they feel about themselves than how they feel about you.

237. Don't let other's negativity pull you down.

238. Learn to be comfortable with yourself even when you're not doing anything.

239. *Learn to be objective so that your past conditioning does not determine your happiness or your misery.*

240. *Know where to draw the line.*

241. *Tell the truth to yourself and to others.*

242. *Sit around a campfire and tell stories.*

243. *Never count on another person for your self-esteem.*

244. *Be independent.*

245. *Establish solid foundations in relationships instead of settling for prefabricated ones.*

246. *Don't be a slave to your upbringing.*

247. *Judge the act, not the person.*

248. Write down all your worries on a sheet of paper, then tear it up and throw it away.

249. Don't make people dependent on you in order to get your own security needs met.

250. Realize that those who hurt you, given their knowledge and circumstances at the time, always act the best they can.

251. *Stop earning the right to be. You achieved that the day you were born.*

252. *Never call yourself names.*

253. *Nurture yourself.*

254. *If you cannot make a situation better, laugh at it instead of yelling at it.*

255. *Ask the wounded child within what he or she needs from you and pay close attention to the answer.*

256. *Sing for yourself as you do chores around the house.*

257. *Get a new hairstyle.*

258. *Learn how to be free while you are downtrodden and you can be free anytime, anywhere.*

259. *Dress to reflect your personality, not someone else's.*

260. *Take off your watch and forget about time for a day.*

261. *Hold your head high instead of looking at the ground.*

262. *Say what's on your mind.*

263. *Find something that you can be passionate and enthusiastic about.*

264. *See light instead of fright at the end of the tunnel.*

265. *Drink a hot cup of milk before bedtime.*

266. *Be flamboyant.*

267. *Play checkers.*

268. *Never settle for second best.*

269. *Learn to let things go as easily as you let them come into your life.*

270. *Go to a park and watch people.*

271. *Express to a true friend what their friendship means to you.*

272. *Sell or give away any clutter in your garage, basement, attic or cellar that you haven't used in five years.*

273. *Let go of any clutter in your mind that no longer serves you.*

274. *Realize that your feelings of inadequacy are inside feelings, not outside reality.*

275. *When someone cuts in front of you in line, tell them how you feel.*

276. *Remember that "Guru" is spelled "Gee You Are You."*

277. *Leave a positive affirmation for yourself on your answering machine.*

278. *Accept your age proudly and gracefully.*

279. *Have priorities and set goals.*

280. *Don't expect something for nothing.*

281. *Be willing to do the work it takes to feel good about yourself.*

282. *Fly a flag that represents something of which you are proud.*

283. *Put a bumper sticker on your car that signifies what you stand for.*

284. *Develop healthy habits.*

285. *Compromise your ideas but never your integrity.*

286. *Identify with positive role models.*

287. *Pick more daisies.*

288. *Participate in community affairs.*

289. *Live by the motto "Things always work out for the best."*

290. *Be honest even when it's painful. It can save you greater hurt in the end.*

READER/CUSTOMER CARE SURVEY

We care about your opinions. Please take a moment to fill out this Reader Survey card and mail it back to us.
As a special **"thank you"** we'll send you exciting news about interesting books and a valuable **Gift Certificate.**

Please PRINT using ALL CAPS

First
Name _____ MI. _____ Last
Name _____

Address _____ City _____

ST _____ Zip _____ Email: _____

Phone # (_____) _____ Fax # (_____) _____

(1) Gender:

_____Female _____Male

(2) Age:

_____12 or under _____40-59

_____13-19 _____60+

_____20-39

(3) What attracts you most to a book?

(Please rank 1-4 in order of preference.)

	1	2	3	4
3) Title	O	O	O	O
4) Cover Design	O	O	O	O
5) Author	O	O	O	O
6) Content	O	O	O	O

(7) Where do you usually buy books?

*Please fill in your top **TWO** choices.*

1)_____Bookstore

2)_____Religious Bookstore

3)_____Online

4)_____Book Club/Mail Order

5)_____Price Club (Costco, Sam's Club, etc.)

6)_____Retail Store (Target, Wal-Mart, etc.)

Comments:

_____

_____

_____

_____

_____

_____

BUSINESS REPLY MAIL
FIRST-CLASS MAIL PERMIT NO 45 DEERFIELD BEACH, FL

POSTAGE WILL BE PAID BY ADDRESSEE

HEALTH COMMUNICATIONS, INC.
3201 SW 15TH STREET
DEERFIELD BEACH FL 33442-9875

291. *Kick up your heels.*

292. *Put all of yourself into your work and your play.*

293. *Let yourself feel instead of taking a pill.*

294. *Build spiritual practices into your daily routines.*

295. *Remind yourself that you're one of a kind and there will never be another you.*

296. *Express joy.*

297. *Realize that your suffering comes from your mental outlook. Change your outlook and you change your life.*

298. *Swallow your pride and ask for help when you need it.*

299. *Stand firm on what you believe in, especially when others who don't agree try to sway you.*

300. *Don't use alcohol and other drugs to boost your self-esteem.*

301. *Don't let past experiences define who you are today.*

302. *Practice random acts of kindness.*

303. *Have healthy outlets for your anger.*

304. *Indulge yourself by getting a massage.*

305. *Cool off before taking your anger out on your loved ones.*

306. Look before your leap.

307. Think before you speak or act.

308. Get all the facts before jumping to conclusions.

309. Put fresh-cut flowers by your bed.

310. Consult with others but always make your own decisions.

311. When you make a mistake, don't treat yourself as if you are the mistake.

312. Give compliments freely to others.

313. Get out of your own way so that you can be all that you can be.

314. Jump on a pogo stick.

315. Travel to new places.

316. *Close your eyes and go inside yourself at least once a day.*

317. *Go out of your way to do a kind deed.*

318. *Don't cut off your nose to spite your face.*

319. *Cheerfully move through your life without a weight on your mind or a worry in your heart.*

320. *Try not to take your successes or your failures too seriously.*

321. *Don't let the fear of an upcoming event fill your mind before the day has arrived.*

322. *Focus on your strengths, not your weaknesses.*

323. *Cast your fate to the wind.*

324. Realize that when you deliberately hurt someone else, you always hurt yourself.

325. Don't equate career success with personal success.

326. Learn to let go of painful experiences in your mind once they have passed instead of living them over and over.

327. *Think the best instead of the worst.*

328. *Give someone flowers for no special reason except to say, "I love you."*

329. *Take responsibility, instead of blaming others, for the condition of your life.*

330. *Pay attention to what your dreams reveal.*

331. Apologize or say "I love you" to anyone with whom you have unfinished business.

332. Live your life to the fullest so that you'll never have any regrets.

333. Always help those you can and don't harm anybody.

334. Realize that fear is only an illusion that keeps us from seeing our true selves.

335. Establish healthy rituals, such as quiet reflections, while you have a hot drink in the mornings.

336. Celebrate birthdays and anniversaries.

337. *Look into the eyes of children to remember the joy and excitement of being alive.*

338. *Look yourself eye to eye in the mirror and tell yourself that you are loving and lovable.*

339. *Do something for someone else without any expectations or rewards.*

340. *Have lunch with a friend.*

341. Seize every moment and live it fully.

342. Leave work at the office instead of taking it to bed.

343. Read something inspirational daily.

344. When something is bothering you, take the time to go within and figure out what it is.

345. *Always be who you are instead of who others want you to be.*

346. *Spend quality time with yourself.*

347. *Pamper yourself by soaking in a long, hot bath.*

348. *Ask for what you need.*

349. *Try to see where your anger comes from.*

350. *Think the best instead of the worst.*

351. Unpack the baggage of an old relationship instead of carrying it into a new one.

352. Climb more mountains, swim more rivers and watch more sunsets.

353. Put up signs and posters in your bedroom and office that lift your spirits and brighten your day.

354. *Take up aerobics, karate or any activity that makes you sweat.*

355. *Never eat junk food from vending machines.*

356. *Listen to soft music and let your mind drift.*

357. *Have a life outside the office.*

358. *To thine own self be true.*

359. Don't take loved ones for granted.

360. Plan to spend a small part of your day with nature, working in a garden or bird-watching.

361. Be romantic.

362. Start a savings account that you will use to splurge at a future date.

363. *Don't let the fear of making mistakes prevent you from pursuing your dreams. Everybody makes mistakes once in a while.*

364. *When you are upset, write down your feelings to get them out.*

365. *Realize that all our troubles stem from our inability to sit alone in a room quietly.*

366. *Learn to listen to and act on your deepest feelings.*

367. *Embrace all parts of yourself — your generosity and selfishness; your kind and mean side.*

368. *Don't label your feelings as "good" or "bad," just accept them all as valid.*

369. *Start to see yourself as a spiritual being having a physical experience, instead of a physical being having a spiritual experience.*

370. *Let go of whatever you've been resisting in your life lately.*

371. *Don't just believe in miracles, expect them.*

372. *Gaze at the stars.*

373. Approach upsetting situations with love instead of anger.

374. Make a list of all the persons you have harmed and make amends to them.

375. Visit a retirement home.

376. Treat your body as if it is a temple that houses an important treasure.

377. *Realize that you are more than your thoughts and feelings; these are just things you have.*

378. *Be compassionate.*

379. *Get involved in social concerns and political issues that are important to you.*

380. *Spend time with people who have similar interests and beliefs.*

381. *When you're in a bad mood and feel that it will last forever, remind yourself that this, too, shall pass.*

382. *Don't be too hard on yourself.*

383. *Easy does it.*

384. *Take your mask off once in a while and let someone know who you really are.*

385. *Dress in a Halloween costume and go trick-or-treating.*

386. *Put your energies into areas where you can make a difference.*

387. *Have a party and play charades.*

388. *Work through deep-seated feelings of guilt and shame because they work against you, not for you.*

389. Take a class or learn a new skill or craft.

390. Accept yourself first before you can be acceptable to others.

391. See negative experiences as opportunities for you to grow.

392. Be as willing to take orders as you are to give them.

393. *Play in the snow.*

394. *If you think of yourself as worthless, change this erroneous belief.*

395. *Eliminate victimizing words such as "can't" or "have to" from your vocabulary.*

396. *When you are feeling abandoned, spend time with yourself.*

397. *Believe that you are enough.*

398. *Put special cards and notes from friends on a bulletin board as a reminder of your worth.*

399. *Try a new form of art through which you can express your innermost feelings.*

400. *Cleanse your mind of all worries of the future and anxieties of the past; do something that puts you fully in the present.*

401. *Turn roadblocks into stepping stones.*

402. *Face your feelings and feel them completely.*

403. *Avoid clinging to anyone or anything.*

404. *Treat yourself to your favorite restaurant.*

405. *If you don't have a favorite restaurant, find one and then treat yourself.*

406. *Let go of other people's opinions and have your own.*

407. *Follow the advice of Abe Lincoln, "Most folks are as happy as they make up their minds to be."*

408. *Define yourself by who you are on the inside, not by what you do.*

409. *Take your own advice.*

410. Have more real troubles and fewer imaginary ones.

411. Be able to tell the difference between new emotional pain and old emotional pain.

412. Ride a merry-go-round.

413. Detach from the chaos of others and choose peace instead.

414. *Do good things for others without thinking of what you will get in return.*

415. *Work in harmony with the world by finding it within yourself first.*

416. *Take your next trip without a thermometer, hot water bottle, umbrella and raincoat.*

417. *Follow your heart when it disagrees with your head.*

418. *Look in the mirror and tell yourself that you're looking at the only person in the world who can stand in the way of your happiness.*

419. *Remember that your mind is like a parachute; it only works when open.*

420. *Don't let the same thoughts and feelings that directed you as a child direct you as an adult.*

421. *Give up trying to please everyone, because no matter which direction you face, you must turn your back on one-half of the world.*

422. *Take life in your hands and, as Leo Buscaglia suggests, "You can select joy if you want or you can find despair everywhere you look."*

423. Give compliments freely.

424. Learn to accept compliments as freely as you give them.

425. Let your emotions serve you instead of letting them rule you.

426. Dwell on happiness instead of despair.

427. *Learn the difference between self-care, self-neglect and self-seeking.*

428. *Be on the cutting edge, but don't fall off.*

429. *When a dark cloud hangs over you, be kind enough to give it a humorous lining.*

430. *Share your feelings with someone else who will benefit by them.*

431. *Turn what you have into enough.*

432. *Live by the adage "We who are content with little possess everything."*

433. *Do some soul-searching.*

434. *Find peace within yourself instead of searching for someone else to complete you.*

435. *Be a liver of life instead of a survivor of it.*

436. Let good feelings become as habitual as the bad ones have.

437. Start barefooted earlier in the spring and stay that way in the fall.

438. Let God pass through you like current through a wire.

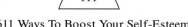
439. *When you fall down, pick yourself up, dust yourself off and keep on going.*

440. *Don't wait for someone else to be joyful before expressing joy yourself.*

441. *Avoid character assassinations.*

442. *If you have the need to assassinate someone's character, examine what it is about yourself that this behavior distracts you from.*

443. *Release your resentments and replace them with love and forgiveness.*

444. *Never make others responsible for your happiness.*

445. *Keep the focus on your inner development no matter where you work, reside or vacation.*

446. *Limber up.*

447. *Live by the moment, instead of living so many years ahead of each day.*

448. *When you are discouraged by how far you have to go, look at how far you have already come.*

449. *Don't force your will on people and situations; it will never work.*

450. *Practice being flexible and spontaneous.*

451. *Feel the fear and do it anyway.*

452. *Give yourself permission to be confused, for on the other side of confusion is clarity.*

453. *Have a catharsis. If you don't know what the word means, look it up and have one anyway.*

454. *Make sure your capability to feel hurt matches your capability to experience joy.*

455. *Make New Year's resolutions and stick to them.*

456. *Stop scaring yourself away from actions that can lead to success, happiness and empowerment.*

457. *Be considerate of others, but please only yourself.*

458. *Be lighthearted instead of serious-minded because, according to John Wilcot, "Care to our coffin adds a nail, no doubt, and every grin so merry draws one out."*

459. *Learn through trial and error.*

460. *Don't apologize twice for the same offense because then it becomes an excuse.*

461. *Walk gently through your life, leaving a strong and large footprint.*

462. *Be able to smile when life flows like a song and to feel worthwhile even when everything goes dead wrong.*

463. *Let your friends know that you treasure and appreciate them.*

464. *Know that you are never alone because you always have yourself.*

465. *Heed the wisdom of Honoré de Balzac, who said, "Nothing is a greater impediment to being on good terms with others than being ill at ease with yourself."*

466. *Nip your grandiosity in the bud.*

467. *See your flaws as a diamond that adds to your value rather than subtracts from it.*

468. *Don't let your past contaminate your present.*

469. *Give yourself credit for a job well done.*

470. *Make your disadvantages and handicaps work for you instead of against you.*

471. *Examine your friendships as a reflection of who you think you are inside.*

472. *When you have a choice of being alone or in bad company, choose being alone.*

473. *Ask for help when you need it.*

474. *See the error of your ways.*

475. Don't amplify the success of others into defeat for yourself.

476. Call someone you miss and haven't heard from in a long time.

477. Avoid hiding from life behind work, alcohol or other addictions.

478. Be outrageous!

479. Ask yourself if your habits are taking you into wild rapids or into calm and serene waters.

480. Let go of false pride.

481. Use prevention instead of Band-Aids.

482. Have your own opinions, but be able to take someone else's point of view.

483. *Be able to admit someone else's idea is better than yours without having damaged self-esteem.*

484. *Live today as if it were "the good old days."*

485. *Tell someone you love them, make a confession or mend a relationship.*

486. *Always think of yourself in process because, as Ray Kroc suggests, "When you're green you're growing. When you're ripe, you're rotten."*

487. *Fantasize.*

488. *Gauge your personal growth by how far you've come, not by how much further you have come than someone else.*

489. Wallow in self-action instead of self-pity.

490. Accept people and experiences as they are, not as you want them to be.

491. Vent your rage constructively because, according to Marianne Williamson, "Rage turned inward is called ulcers and cancer and things like that."

492. *When you feel isolated from others, know that it is just a feeling that will run its course.*

493. *Live unhampered by things that are extraneous.*

494. *Acknowledge your own mind, body and spirit and use them to your best advantage.*

495. *Don't believe in Murphy's Law.*

496. *Keep your mind clear and know the direction in which you are headed.*

497. *"Don't bury a hatchet," Sydney Harris advises, "if you are going to put up a marker on the site."*

498. *Live your life the same way a Chihuahua goes about eating a dead elephant: one bite at a time, being very present with that bite.*

499. *When you shake your fist at someone, notice that all your fingers are pointing at yourself.*

500. *Don't tell Sue something about Joe that you need to say to Joe directly.*

501. *Possess things and love people, instead of the other way around.*

502. *Understand that it is okay and even healthy to disagree with another person.*

503. *Avoid snap decisions.*

504. *When things don't go the way you want, first look within for the reason.*

505. *Strive for a well-rounded life.*

506. *Notice the treasures that lurk behind the humdrum, ordinary things in your life.*

507. *Get reacquainted with yourself daily.*

508. *Don't let pettiness distract you from the truly important things.*

509. *Surrender.*

510. Be aware that your actions can affect the lives of others in more ways than you may realize.

511. When you are faced with problems, notice how unexpected events and conversations reveal solutions and answers.

512. Remind yourself that things of value don't come easily; that's what makes them valuable.

513. *Be aware of your powerlessness and you will be empowered.*

514. *Have self-discipline.*

515. *Sweep in front of your own door so that the whole world will be clean.*

516. *Deliberately do something imperfectly.*

517. *Get your mind off the EGO which stands for "Ease God Out."*

518. *Practice compassion.*

519. *Take a wellness day off from work instead of a sick day.*

520. *Release all your self-debasing thoughts and feelings.*

521. *Step aside when you get in the way of your progress.*

522. *On a clear night, find the North Star.*

523. *Surround yourself with beauty inside and out.*

524. *Save yourself a nest egg.*

525. *Have faith in something greater than yourself.*

526. *Don't play with matches and you won't always be putting out fires.*

527. *Ask yourself what you gain from creating crises and get your needs met in more positive ways.*

528. *Be able to admit errors without diminishing your self-esteem.*

529. *Let go of the burden of always being right.*

530. *Choose always being happy over always being right.*

531. *Let constructive pastimes attract you more than lethal ones.*

532. *Use troubles on the job as experiences from which you can learn and grow.*

533. *Admit your wrongs but don't carry a grudge against yourself.*

534. *Rejoice in the good fortune of others.*

535. *Be thankful for your own good fortune.*

536. *Know that you are okay exactly as you are.*

537. *Ask for daily strength and guidance.*

538. *Feel the wind on your face and in your hair.*

539. Choose love over hate.

540. Quiet yourself and notice how much more you hear and see.

541. Be a caregiver instead of a caretaker.

542. Create a feeling of optimism instead of impending doom.

543. Have time for the ones you care about.

544. Notice what you learn though the pain of confronting and resolving your problems.

545. Accept yourself by releasing other people's opinions.

546. Don't sweat the small stuff.

547. Remind yourself often that it's all small stuff.

548. *Support the politics that fit your value system.*

549. *Be kind to children and pets.*

550. *Be zestful instead of fretful.*

551. *Avoid putting others on a pedestal.*

552. *Avoid putting others down.*

553. *Have relationships that feel equal and fair.*

554. *Relax.*

555. *Pay attention to your irrational thoughts that cause you to have irrational feelings.*

556. *Replace irrational thoughts with rational ones.*

557. *Have a Higher Power.*

558. *Refuse to listen to racist, sexist and anti-gay jokes.*

559. *Avoid little white lies.*

560. *Get the facts before jumping to conclusions.*

561. *Don't wait for someone else to make decisions for you.*

562. *Make up your own mind.*

563. *Pay yourself first before paying your bills.*

564. *Learn to feel at home in your own skin.*

565. *Don't judge a book by its cover.*

566. *Listen carefully.*

567. *Concentrate on the truly important things around you from second to second.*

568. *Open new doors instead of trying to get in the old, locked ones.*

569. *Let go of greedy and selfish habits.*

570. *Live by the motto "Yesterday I was, tomorrow I will be and today I am."*

571. *When the bottom falls out, try to see what blessings can be gained from the crisis.*

572. *Be open-minded instead of close-minded.*

573. *Be receptive to everything.*

574. *Practice sharing.*

575. *Heed the words of Lao Tzu who said, "The way to do is to be."*

576. *Rephrase hopeless thoughts into more hopeful ones and say them out loud.*

577. *Have thoughts of prosperity and abundance instead of scarcity and lack.*

578. *Say something nice to someone you've had conflict with.*

579. *Choose exhilaration over misery.*

580. *Use your senses to experience the world as you have never experienced it before.*

581. *Stop to see how important the little things really are.*

582. *Instead of trying to put the world and others in order, put yourself in unison with the order that already exists.*

583. *Empower yourself with your ability to choose what you will think, how you feel and how you will act.*

584. *Depend on others, but don't "co-depend" on them.*

585. *Decide what your outlook on the world will be from one minute to the next.*

586. *Don't make promises you cannot keep.*

587. *Keep the promises you make.*

588. *Never speak for someone else or let someone else speak for you.*

589. *Learn to get through life by facing it instead of hiding from it.*

590. *Don't keep secrets that can harm you.*

591. *Avoid burning the candle at both ends.*

592. *Go out on a limb to get the fruit of the tree.*

593. *When you say you want to be "somebody," acknowledge that you already are "somebody."*

594. *Practice humility.*

595. *Recognize that the same power that governs the moon and stars and makes flowers grow also flows through you.*

596. *Be happy with yourself first before trying to be happy with anyone else.*

597. *Ask for help when you need it.*

598. Reach out to someone else who needs help.

599. Give help only when others want it.

600. Don't give unsolicited advice.

601. When you're helping someone else, don't steal their problem away from them and make it your own.

602. *Have a deep and rich inner life and you will be more successful in dealing with the often agonizing details of your outer life.*

603. *Move at a snail's pace.*

604. *Take stress breaks.*

605. *For today, tackle only the things that demand resolution now and deal with tomorrow, tomorrow.*

606. *Have contact with your spiritual self and your need for approval from others will be replaced with self-approval.*

607. *Don't let the negativity of others pull you down.*

608. *Let go of all the self-ridicule and self-defeating thoughts and feelings you are storing in your head.*

609. *Love and do good things for yourself and that self-love will surely be transferred to others.*

610. *Be grateful for all the good things you already have instead of whining over what you lack.*

611. *Remember the words of T.S. Eliot, who said, "To make an end is to make a beginning. The end is where we start from."*